Barack Obama

© B. Jain Publishers (P) Ltd. All rights reserved. No part of this book may be reproduced, stored in a retrieval system or transmitted, in any form or by any means, mechanical, photocopying, recording or otherwise, without any prior written permission of the publisher.

Published by Kuldeep Jain for B. Jain Publishers (P) Ltd., D-157, Sector 63, Noida - 201307, U.P
Registered office: 1921/10, Chuna Mandi, Paharganj, New Delhi-110055

Printed in India

Contents

5   Who is Barack Obama?

6   Childhood and Early Life

10 Education and Gaining Knowledge

15 Career in Law

18 A Sweet Story of Romance

21 Doorway to Illinois Politics

24 Career in the US Senate

28 2008 Presidential Election

36 Challenges and Successes

53 Timeline

60 Activities

62 Glossary

Who is Barack Obama?

Barack Hussein Obama is the 44th and the current President of the United States. He is the first African-American to hold this office. Before pursuing his political career, Obama was a community organizer, civil-rights lawyer and constitutional law teacher at the University of Chicago Law School.

Obama was elected to the Illinois State Senate in 1996 and to the US Senate in 2004. He served three terms representing the 13th district in the Illinois Senate from 1997 to 2004, running unsuccessfully for the United States House of Representatives in 2000 against Bobby Rush.

Childhood and Early Life

Barack Hussein Obama II was born on August 4, 1961 in Honolulu, Hawaii. He was born to Ann Dunham, a white American from Kansas, and Barack Obama Sr., a black Kenyan studying in the United States. Obama's father left the family when Obama was two and after further studies at Harvard University, returned to Kenya. He died there in an automobile accident nineteen years later. After the divorce of his parents, Obama's mother married another foreign student at the University of Hawaii, Lolo Soetoro of Indonesia. Obama continued to live with his mother and stepfather in Indonesia until he turned 10. There he attended Catholic and Muslim schools. "I was raised as an Indonesian child and a Hawaiian child and as a black child and as a white child," Obama stated during one of his interviews. "And so what I benefited from is a multiplicity of cultures that all fed me."

Obama's father, Barack Obama Sr., was born of Luo ethnicity in Nyanza Province, Kenya. Obama Sr. grew up herding goats in Africa and eventually earned a scholarship that allowed him to leave Kenya and pursue his dreams of going to college in Hawaii. While studying at the University of Hawaii at Manoa, Obama Sr. met fellow student Ann Dunham, and they married on February 2, 1961. Obama was born six months later.

As a child, Obama did not see much of his father. When Obama was still small, his parents officially separated and ultimately filed for a divorce in March 1964. Soon after, Obama Sr. returned to Kenya.

In the year 1965, Obama's mother Ann, married Lolo Soetoro, a student of University of Hawaii who belonged to Indonesia. A year later, the family moved to Jakarta, Indonesia, where Obama's half-sister, Maya Soetoro Ng, was born in 1970. Several incidents in Indonesia made Ann feel insecure of her son's safety and education. Hence, at the age of 10, Obama was sent back to Hawaii to live with his maternal grandparents. His mother and half-sister later joined them.

Education and Gaining Knowledge

While living with his grandparents, Obama enrolled in the esteemed Punahou Academy. There he excelled in basketball and graduated with academic honours in 1979. As one of only three black students in the school, Obama for the first time became conscious

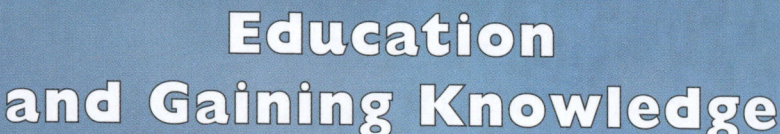

of racism and what it meant to be African-American. He later described how he struggled to reconcile social perceptions of his multiracial heritage with his own sense of self. He once wrote, 'I noticed that there was nobody like me in the Sears, Roebuck Christmas catalog … and that Santa was a white man.' He further added: 'I went into the bathroom and stood in front of the mirror with all my senses and limbs seemingly intact, looking as I had always looked, and wondered if something was wrong with me.'

Young Obama also struggled due to the absence of his father, whom he saw only once after his parents divorced, when Obama Sr. visited Hawaii for a short while in 1971. On one occasion, Obama said about his father: "[My father] had left paradise, and nothing that my mother or grandparents told me could obviate that single, unassailable fact. They couldn't describe what it might have been like had he stayed."

In 1981, ten years later, Obama Sr. lost both of his legs in a serious car accident. Confined to a wheelchair, he also lost his job. In 1982, Obama Sr. met with yet another car accident while travelling in Nairobi. This time, however, the crash was fatal. Obama Sr. died on November 24, 1982, when Obama was 21 years old. 'At the time of his death, my father remained a myth to me,' Obama later wrote. 'Both more and less than a man,' he added. It was indeed sad for Obama, who never came in contact with his father his entire life!

After high school, Obama studied at Occidental College in Los Angeles for two years. He was then transferred to Columbia University in New York City, where he finished his graduation in 1983 with a degree in political science. After working in the business sector for two years, Obama moved to Chicago in 1985. While in Chicago, he worked on the impoverished South Side as a community organizer for low-income residents in the Roseland and Altgeld Gardens communities.

Career in Law

It was during this time that Obama visited his relatives in Kenya and paid an emotional visit to the graves of his biological father and paternal grandfather. 'For a long time I sat between the two graves and wept,' Obama wrote. 'I saw that my life in America—the black life, the white life, the sense of abandonment I'd felt as a boy, the frustration and hope I'd witnessed in Chicago—all of it was connected with this small plot of earth an ocean away.'

Returning from Kenya with a sense of rejuvenation, Obama entered Harvard Law School in 1988. The next year, he joined the Chicago law firm of Sidley Austin as a summer associate and Michelle Robinson, a young lawyer assigned to be Obama's adviser. Not long after, the couple began dating. In February 1990, Obama was elected the first African-American editor of the Harvard Law Review. He graduated with great distinction from Harvard in 1991.

After law school, Obama returned to Chicago to practice as a civil rights lawyer with the firm of Miner, Barnhill & Galland. He also taught constitutional law part-time at the University of Chicago Law School between 1992 and 2004, first as a lecturer and then as a professor. He also helped organize voter registration drives during Bill Clinton's 1992 presidential campaign.

A Sweet
Story of Romance

How Obama met his wife is an interesting story. Michelle LaVaughn Robinson Obama is an American lawyer and writer. She was raised on the South Side of Chicago and is a graduate of Princeton University and Harvard Law School.

After attending the law school, Michelle worked as an associate in the Chicago branch of the law firm Sidley Austin in the area of marketing and intellectual property. There, in 1989, she met her future husband, Obama, a summer intern to whom she was assigned as an adviser.

Though Obama was not too fond of the corporate law world, he soon found himself falling for Michelle. "We clicked right away … by the end of the date it was over … I was sold," remembers the First Lady fondly. She also said, "Barack didn't pledge riches; only a life that would be interesting. On that promise he delivered."

Initially, she refused to date Obama, believing that their work relationship would make the romance improper. Eventually, she relented, and the couple soon fell deep in love with each other.

After two years of dating, Obama proposed marriage to Michelle. The couple married at Trinity United Church of Christ on October 3, 1992. Their daughters, Malia and Sasha, were born in 1998 and 2001, respectively.

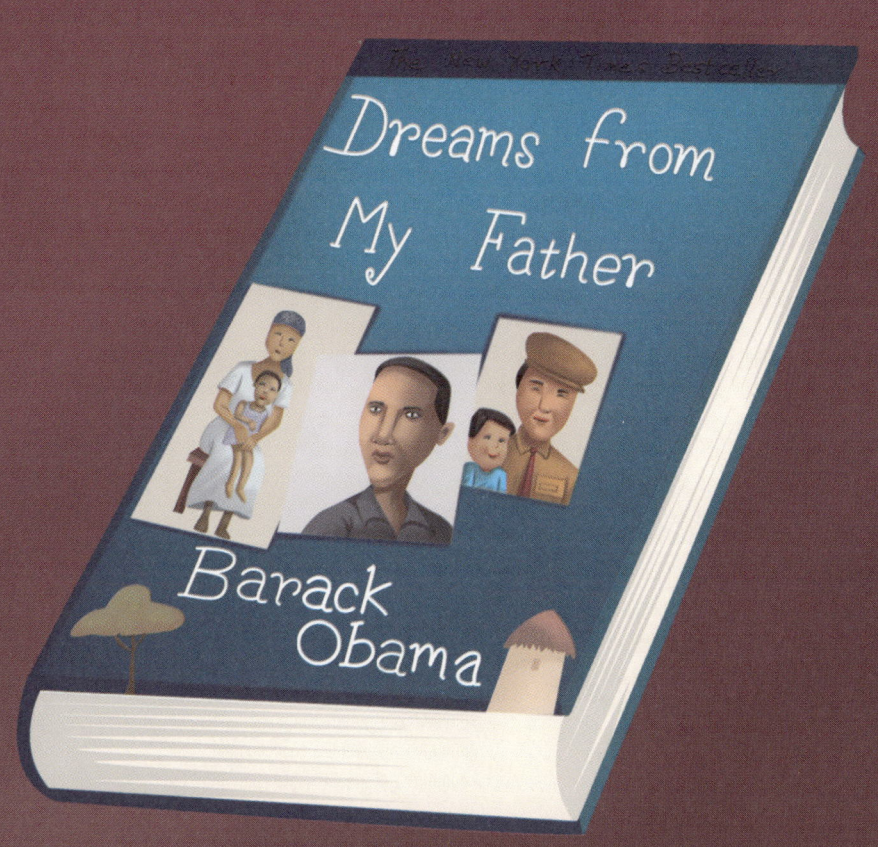

Doorway to Illinois Politics

In the year 1995, Obama published an autobiography titled, Dreams from My Father: A Story of Race and Inheritance. The work received high admiration from the literary world and has since been printed in more than 25 languages, including Chinese, Swedish and Hebrew. The book was sent for reprint in 2004, and it was adapted for a children's version. The audio version of the book, narrated by Obama, received a Grammy for best spoken word album in 2006.

Obama's advocacy work led him to contest for a seat in the Illinois State Senate. He fought as a Democrat and won the election in 1996. During his years as a state senator, Obama worked with both Democrats and Republicans to draft legislation on ethics, as well as expand health care services and early childhood education programmes for the poor. He also created a state-earned income tax credit for the working poor. As the chairman of the Illinois Senate's Health and Human Services Committee, Obama worked with law enforcement officials to require the videotaping of interrogations and confessions in all capital cases after a number of death-row inmates were found to be innocent.

In 2000, Obama made an unsuccessful primary contest for the US House of Representatives seat held by Bobby Rush, who was in office for four-terms. Undeterred, Obama created a campaign committee in 2002 and began raising funds to contest for a seat in the US Senate in 2004. With the help of political consultant David Axelrod, Obama began assessing his prospects for a Senate victory.

Career in the US Senate

Encouraged by poll numbers, Obama decided to run for the US Senate open seat vacated by Republican Peter Fitzgerald. In the 2004 Democratic primary, he defeated the multimillionaire businessman Blair Hull and Illinois Comptroller Daniel Hynes with 52 per cent of the vote. That summer, he was invited to deliver the keynote

speech in support of John Kerry at the 2004 Democratic National Convention in Boston.

After the convention, Obama returned to his US Senate bid in Illinois. His opponent in the general election was supposed to be Republican primary winner Jack Ryan, a wealthy former investment banker. However, Ryan withdrew from the election in June 2004 following

public disclosure of unconfirmed sexual deviancy allegations by his ex-wife, actress Jeri Ryan.

In August 2004, diplomat and former presidential candidate Alan Keyes accepted the Republican nomination to replace Ryan. In three televised debates, Obama and Keyes expressed opposing views on stem cell research, abortion, gun control, school vouchers and tax cuts. In the November 2004 general election, Obama received 70 per cent of the votes to Keyes' 27 percent, the largest electoral victory in the history of Illinois. With this win, Obama became only the third African-American elected to the US Senate since Reconstruction. He was sworn in to office on January 3, 2005.

2008 Presidential Election

Obama made headlines when he announced his candidacy for the 2008 Democratic presidential nomination in February 2007. He was engaged in a tight battle with former first lady and then US senator from New York,

Hillary Rodham Clinton. On June 3, 2008, Obama became the Democratic Party's presumptive nominee after winning a sufficient number of pledged delegates during the primaries, and Hillary delivered her full support to Obama during his campaign. On November 4, 2008, Obama defeated Republican presidential nominee John McCain by 52.9 per cent to 45.7 per cent.

Obama won the election and became the 44th President of the United States. He is the first African-American to hold this office. His running mate, Delaware Senator Joe Biden, became vice president. Obama's inaugural ceremony took place on January 20, 2009.

Alongside assuming office, Obama inherited a global economic recession and two ongoing foreign wars. He campaigned on financial reforms, alternative energy and reinventing education and health care—all while bringing down the national debt. As all these issues were intertwined with the economic well being of the nation, he believed all would have to be undertaken simultaneously. During his inauguration speech, Obama summarized the situation by saying, "Today I say to you that the challenges we face are real. They are serious and they are many. They will not be met easily or in a short span of time. But know this, America: They will be met."

This showed how promising and confident he was from the very beginning.

Over his first 100 days in office, President Obama also undertook a complete revamp of America's foreign policy.
He reached out to improve relations with Europe, China and Russia, and to open dialogue with Iran, Venezuela and Cuba. He committed an additional 21,000 troops to Afghanistan and set an August 2010 date for withdrawal of nearly all US troops from

Iraq. In more dramatic incidents, he ordered an attack on pirates off the coast of Somalia and prepared the nation for a swine flu outbreak. For his efforts, the Nobel Committee in Norway awarded Obama the 2009 Nobel Peace Prize.

On January 27, 2010, President Obama delivered his first State of the Union speech. During his oration, Obama addressed the challenges of the economy. He also challenged politicians to stop thinking of re-election and start making positive changes. He also insisted that, despite obstacles, he was determined to help American citizens through the nation's domestic difficulties. "We don't quit. I don't quit," he said. 'Let's seize this moment to start anew, to carry the dream forward, and to strengthen our union once more."

Challenges and Successes

The road to presidentship has not been an easy one for Obama. He faced a number of obstacles and scored some victories and many criticisms. In spite of opposition from Congressional Republicans and the populist Tea Party Movement, Obama signed his health care reform plan, known as the Affordable Care Act, into law in March 2010. The new law prohibited the denial of coverage based on pre-existing conditions allowed citizens under 26 years old to be insured under parental plans, provided for free health screenings for certain citizens and expanded insurance coverage and access to medical care to millions of Americans.

On the economic front, Obama worked very hard to steer his country through difficult financial times. He signed the Budget Control Act of 2011 in an effort to rein in government spending and prevent the government from defaulting on its financial obligations. This act also created a bipartisan committee to seek solutions to the country's fiscal issues, but the group failed to reach any agreement on how to solve these problems.

During his campaign for a second presidential term, Obama focused on grassroots initiatives as he did in 2008. Celebrities such as Anna Wintour and Sarah Jessica Parker aided the president's campaign by hosting fund-raising events.

"I guarantee you; we will move this country forward," Obama stated in June 2012, at a campaign event in Maryland. "We will finish what we started. And we'll remind the world just why it is that the United States of America is the greatest nation on Earth."

Obama faced Republican opponent Mitt Romney in the 2012 election. On November 6, 2012, Obama won a second 'four-year term' as president by receiving nearly

five million more votes than Romney and capturing more than 60 per cent of the Electoral College.

Obama officially began his second term on January 21, 2013, when US Chief Justice John Roberts administered the oath of office. The inauguration was held on Martin Luther King Jr. Day, and civil rights activist Myrlie Evers-Williams, the widow of Medgar Evers, gave the invocation. James Taylor, Beyoncé Knowles and Kelly Clarkson sang

at the ceremony, and poet Richard Blanco read his poem One Today.

In his inaugural address, Obama called the nation to take action on such issues as climate change, health care and marriage equality. After the inauguration, Obama led the nation through many challenges. The most difficult one was perhaps the terrorist bombings of the Boston Marathon on April 15, 2013, which killed three people

and left more than 200 injured. At a memorial service in Boston three days after the bombings, Obama told the injured, "Your country is with you. We will all be with you as you learn to stand and walk and, yes, run again. Of that I have no doubt. You will run again." He further commended the city's response to the tragedy saying, 'You've shown us, Boston, that in the face of evil, Americans will lift up what's good. In the face of cruelty, we will choose compassion.'

In early July 2013, President Obama created history when he joined former President George W. Bush in Africa to commemorate the 15th anniversary of Al-Qaeda's first attack on American targets, the US embassies in Tanzania and Kenya. The event marked the first meeting between two US presidents on foreign soil in commemoration of an act of terrorism.

Apart from the challenges faced at home, Obama found himself surrounded with an international crisis in late

August and September 2013, when it was discovered that Syrian leader Bashar al-Assad had used chemical weapons against civilians. While saying that thousands of people, including over 400 children, had been killed in the chemical attacks, Obama called Syria's actions as, "A serious national security threat to the United States and to the region, and as a consequence, Assad and Syria needs to be held accountable."

The president persuaded the Congress and the international community at large to take action against Syria but found a majority on Capitol Hill being opposed to military involvement. Obama then announced an alternative solution on September 10, 2013, by stating that if Al-Assad agreed with the conditions outlined in a proposal made by Russia to give up its chemical weapons, then a direct strike against the nation could be avoided. Al-Assad acknowledged the possession of chemical weapons and ultimately accepted the Russian proposal.

Later that month, Obama made diplomatic strides with Iran. He spoke with the Iranian President Hassan Rouhani on the phone which marked the first direct contact between the leaders of the two countries in more than 30 years. This groundbreaking move by Obama was seen by many as a sign of thawing in the relationship between the United States and Iran. "The two of us discussed our ongoing efforts to reach an agreement over Iran's nuclear program," reported Obama at a press conference in which he expressed optimism that a deal could be reached to lift sanctions on Iran in return for that country's willingness to halt its nuclear development programme.

The fall of 2013 brought Obama additional challenges in the area of foreign relations. In October 2013, German Chancellor Angela Merkel revealed that the National Security Association of U.S (NSA) had been listening in to her cell phone calls. "Spying among friends is never acceptable," Merkel told a summit of European leaders. In the wake of these controversies, Obama saw his approval rating drop to a new low in November 2013. Only 37 per cent of Americans polled by CBS News approved of the job he was doing as the president, while 57 per cent disapproved of his handling of the job.

Echoes of the Cold War also returned after civil unrest and protests in the capital city of Kiev led to the downfall of Ukrainian President Viktor Yanukovych's administration in February 2014. Russian troops crossed into Ukraine to support pro-Russian forces and the annexation of the province of Crimea. In response to this, Obama ordered sanctions targeting individuals and businesses considered by the US government to be Ukraine agitators or involved in the Crimean crisis.

In August 2014, Obama ordered the first airstrikes against the self-proclaimed Islamic state, also known as ISIS or ISIL, which had seized large parts of Iraq and Syria and conducted high-profile beheadings of foreign hostages. The following month, the US launched its first attacks on ISIS targets in Syria. Several Arab countries joined in the airstrikes against the extremist Islamic militant group. "The only language understood by killers like this is the language of force," Obama said in a speech to the United Nations.

In his 2015 State of the Union address, Obama declared that the nation was out of recession. "America, for all that we've endured; for all the grit and hard work required to come back ... know this: The shadow of crisis has passed," he said in an assuring tone. He went on to share his vision for ways to improve the nation through free community college programmes and middle-class tax breaks.

Not long after his State of the Union address, Obama travelled to India to meet Prime Minister Narendra Modi. According to several news reports, Obama and Modi had reached a breakthrough understanding regarding India's nuclear power efforts. Obama told the Indian people in a speech given in New Delhi, "We can finally move toward fully implementing our civil nuclear agreement, which will mean more reliable electricity for Indians and cleaner, non-carbon energy that helps fight climate change." This agreement would also open the door to US investment in India's energy industry.

Perhaps the biggest triumph of Obama's presidency came on May 2, 2011, when Navy SEALs and CIA operatives shot and killed Osama bin Laden in Abbottabad, Pakistan. The operation was a risky one for Obama. Despite months of intelligence work leading up to the raid, there was no guarantee that Laden would be in the compound. The risk paid off when the world's most wanted terrorist was finally killed nearly 10 years after the September 11, 2001 terrorist attacks.

A month after Laden was killed, Obama announced that the US had largely achieved its goals in Afghanistan and that time had come to start withdrawing troops and begin "to focus on nation-building here at home." On December 15, 2011, Obama declared that the US-led war in Iraq had officially ended. The war, launched in March 2003, lasted nearly nine years, killed more than 4,440 U.S. troops, and cost about US$ 1 trillion!

Obama's story is today the story of America, which consists of values from the heart, a middle-class upbringing in a strong family, hard work and education as the means of getting ahead!

- 1961 Barack Obama, Sr., a Kenyan, and Stanley (Ann) Dunham, an American, marry in Maui, in February.

    Barack Jr. is born in August in Honolulu, Hawaii.

    Ann takes Barack Jr. with her to attend the University of Washington in Seattle.

- 1962 Obama Sr. moves to Harvard to study economics on receiving a graduate scholarship.

    Ann returns to the University of Hawaii, where she meets Lolo Soetoro, an exchange student from Indonesia.

- 1964 Obama Jr. spends much time with his maternal grandparents while his mother attends college.

    Ann files for and receives a divorce from Obama Sr.

- 1965 Ann marries Soetoro.
- 1966 Soetoro returns to Jakarta, Indonesia.
- 1967 Ann and Obama Jr. move to Soetero's hometown in Jakarta, Indonesia.
- 1970 Soetoro and Ann have a daughter, Maya.

Timeline

- **1971** When Obama Jr. turns 10, he is sent back to Hawaii to live with his maternal grandparents.

    His father, Barack Sr., comes to Hawaii for a visit.

- **1972** Ann returns to Hawaii with her daughter Maya and attends graduate studies at the University of Hawaii.

- **1975** Ann returns to Indonesia for carrying out a field work on her Ph.D. in anthropology.

    Barack Jr. stays back in Honolulu with his grandparents.

    He attends school at Punahou, a prestigious prep school in Hawaii.

- **1979** Barack Jr. starts attending Occidental College in Los Angeles.

- **1980** Ann divorces Soetoro.

- **1981** Obama Jr. makes his first public speech, stating that Occidental should support the abolishment of apartheid in South Africa.

    He is transferred to Columbia University in order to major in political science.

Timeline

- **1982** Obama Sr. dies in a car accident in Kenya.

- **1983** Obama Jr. graduates from Columbia with a Bachelor of Arts degree.

- **1988** Obama Jr. begins to study at Harvard Law School. After his first year, he begins working as an intern for a top law firm located in Chicago. It is here that meets the woman who he would eventually marry.

- **1990** Obama Jr. becomes the first black president of the Harvard Law Review.

- **1991** Obama Jr. graduates from Harvard with his law degree and begins working on his book, Dreams of My Father.

- **1992** He becomes the director of Illinois Project Vote.

    Obama begins teaching constitutional law at the University of Chicago Law School.

    Ann earns her Ph.D. in anthropology from the University of Hawaii.

    Obama Jr. marries Michelle Robinson.

- **1993** Obama Jr. shows interest in issues

Timeline

related to race and poverty. While still teaching, he starts working with the Developing Communities Project as a community organizer.

He joins a law firm that specialized in civil rights legislation.

- 1995 His mother returns to Hawaii; she is diagnosed with cancer.

  Ann dies at the age of 52 from ovarian and uterine cancer.

  Dreams of My Father is published.

- 1996 Obama Jr. is elected to the Illinois Senate.

- 1998 Obama's first daughter, Malia Ann, is born.

- 1999 Obama Jr. runs for Congress but loses to the Republican Bobby Rush.

- 2001 Obama's second daughter Natasha (Sasha) is born.

- 2002 He begins campaigning for the United States Senate.

- 2003 He becomes the chairman of the Illinois Senate's Health and Human Services Committee.

- 2004　Obama gives a keynote speech at the Democratic National Convention.

　　　　He is elected to the United States Senate.

- 2005　Obama is sworn in as a U.S. Senator.

- 2007　He announces his candidacy to be President of the United States.

- 2008　Obama's grandmother passes away.

　　　　It is announced that he beat Hillary Clinton in the primary race for the presidency and received the presidential nomination of the Democratic Party primary election.

　　　　In November, it is announced that Obama has defeated Republican John McCain in the general election and that he would be the next president.

- 2009　Obama is inaugurated as 44th President of the United States.

　　　　US$ 787 billion Economic Stimulus Bill is signed into Law.

　　　　Obama is awarded the Nobel Peace Prize.

Timeline

- **2010** The Patient Protection and Affordable Care Act (Obama Care) is passed.

   BP oil rig explosion takes place in the Gulf of Mexico.

   The Compromise tax plan is passed extending the tax cuts initiated by George W. Bush

- **2011** Osama bin Laden is killed in a US raid in Pakistan.

   Libyan leader Colonel Qaddaffi is killed.

   Islamic militants attack the American diplomatic compound.

- **2012** Obama is re-elected to a second term as President, defeating Mitt Romney.

   Obama begins his second term as the U.S. President.

   The No Budget, No Pay Act of 2013 is signed into law.

- **2013** The Violence Against Women Act is signed into law

   Terrorist forces in Iraq and Syria merge to create the Islamic State in Iraq and the Levant (ISIL) reflecting the new goal of territorial ownership of all of Iraq and the Levant (Syria and Lebanon).

The Freedom Tower (One World Trade Center) was completed in July 2013 and opened November 3, 2014

- 2013 The Boston Marathon bombing terrorist attack takes place in April.
- 2014 Obama meets with the Dalai Lama at the White House.

    Russian military intervention in Ukraine begins.

    The President visits troops and military leaders at Bagram Airfield in Afghanistan.

Activities

Research Activity

Presidents' Day is a holiday honouring the past presidents of the United States. Do your own research and find out the history behind Presidents' Day. Make a report on the history of this day and fill in details like when is it celebrated, what happens on this day and how did it come into being!

Make Your Own Book

Here is a list of five presidents of America. Look up the Internet, search in libraries and check out old magazine and newspapers to find out information about any one of the presidents and make your own scrapbook on them. Deal every aspect of their life separately. Divide the matter into chapters and also paste pictures. Do not forget to make a book jacket for your scrapbook on which you would write the book's name. Here is the list:

Abraham Lincoln
1861-1865

Franklin Delano Roosevelt
1933-1945

John F. Kennedy
1961-1963

Theodore Roosevelt
1901-1909

Woodrow Wilson
1913-1921

Questions

1. Who is Barack Obama?
2. When and where was he born?
3. Who were his parents?
4. Where did Obama study in his childhood?
5. What did he realize about racism?
6. Why did Obama not have time with his father?
7. Name the college in which Obama studied.
8. Where did Obama study law?
9. How and where did Obama meet his wife?
10. When did they get married?
11. Name the autobiography of Obama.
12. When was Obama elected in the US Senate?
13. When did he win the presidential election?
14. Why is Obama considered to be a special president among all others?
15. How many terms did he serve?
16. Mention one incident in which Obama was particularly successful.

Glossary

admiration: respect and warm approval for somebody or something

annexation: the action of annexing something

anniversary: the date on which an event took place

beheading: the action of cutting off a person's head

civil rights: the rights of citizens to political and social freedom, and equality

commemorate: to remember and show respect for someone or something

community: a group of people having a particular characteristic in common or living in the same place

constitutional law: the body of law which defines the relationship of different entities within a state—the executive, the legislature, and the judiciary

death-row: a block or section in the prison for those sentenced to death

Democrats: a supporter of democracy

denial: the act of denying something

deviancy: to diverge from usual or accepted standards

Glossary

disapprove: an unfavourable opinion

disclosure: to make new or secret information known

effort: a vigorous attempt to do something

ethnicity: belonging to a social group that has a common national or cultural tradition

fiscal: relating to government revenue

groundbreaking: innovative

hostages: a person held as security for the fulfillment of some condition

improve: to become better

inauguration: the beginning or introduction of any system

intertwined: twist or twine together

legislation: laws considered collectively

marathon: a long-distance running race

memorial: a statue or structure established to remind people of a person or an incident

multiracial: made up of or related to people of many races

part-time: for only part of the usual working day

paternal: belonging to the father's side

Glossary

perceptions: the ability to see, hear, or become aware of something

persuaded: to induce someone to do something through reasoning

prohibit: something that has been forbidden

proposal: a plan or suggestion put forward in a formal or written form

reconcile: to restore friendly relations

revamp: give new and improved form of something

scholarship: a grant or payment made to support a student's education

screenings: to show a film, video, or television programme

seize: to hold something suddenly and forcibly

swine flu: a form of influenza

terrorism: the unofficial or unauthorized use of violence

unconfirmed: not confirmed as valid

undeterred: persevering with something despite setbacks